all about lizards

by robert g. sprackland, jr.

COVER: Above: *Eumeces laticeps,* southeastern United States. Photo by F.J. Dodd, Jr. Below: *Lacerta lepida,* northwestern Africa and southwestern Europe. Photo by H. Hansen, Aquarium Berlin.

FRONTIS: *Phelsuma madagascariensis,* the Madagascar day gecko. Photo by H. Hansen, Aquarium Berlin.

ISBN 0-87666-906-2

Distributed in the U.S.A. by T.F.H. Publications, Inc., 211 West Sylvania Avenue, P.O. Box 27, Neptune City, N.J. 07753; in England by T.F.H. (Gt. Britain) Ltd., 13 Nutley Lane, Reigate, Surrey; in Canada to the book store and library trade by Clarke, Irwin & Company, Clarwin House, 791 St. Clair Avenue West, Toronto 10, Ontario; in Canada to the pet trade by Rolf C. Hagen Ltd., 3225 Sartelon Street, Montreal 382, Quebec; in Southeast Asia by Y.W. Ong, 9 Lorong 36 Geylang, Singapore 14; in Australia and the south Pacific by Pet Imports Pty. Ltd., P.O. Box 149, Brookvale 2100, N.S.W., Australia. Published by T.F.H. Publications, Inc. Ltd., The British Crown Colony of Hong Kong.

Contents

The tokay gecko, *Gekko gecko,* is a large southern Asian species carried around the world by commerce. It is commonly found around houses and does well in captivity. Photo by H. Hansen, Aquarium Berlin.

Only male yellow-headed geckos (*Gonatodes albigularis fuscus*) have the yellow head, the females being more somberly colored. This three-inch specimen is from Key West, Florida. Photo by J.T. Collins.

The brilliant South American *Gonatodes ceciliae*, like other *Gonatodes*, lacks the toe pads typical of most geckos. Photo by J.D. Hardy, courtesy U.S. National Mus.

Acknowledgments

I would like to thank the many people who contributed to the completion of this book.

I extend my thanks to Drs. Herndon Dowling, Frederick B. Turner and Hymen Marx for use of materials and facilities at their disposal. For specimens I am indebted to Dr. Wolfgang Bohme, Benedict Sandin and David Brownlee. Dr. Robert Mertens and Dr. Donald Broadley kindly supplied data on unusual lizards.

I thank Dr. George Zug of the U.S. National Museum for allowing me to examine the rare *Shinisaurus* in his care and for the excellent photographs. Mr. Joseph T. Collins did an excellent job with the photographs and helped in other ways. For hours spent helping me locate obscure material in libraries as well as the field, my deep thanks to Messers. Michael Cheung, John Flanagan, and Miss Teri Carlson. Mr. Chip E. Miller translated some valuable material from German. To Miss Lynette Abra and Mr. Eric Worrell of the Australian Reptile Park, I convey my appreciation for information and excellent photographs.

My family, Captain and Mrs. Joseph Smith, Miss Marilyn Badaracco, and Mrs. V.J. Badaracco have offered support and invaluable assistance in every way. In particular, I want to thank three good friends without whose interest and support this project would still be a far off dream: Dr. Samuel B. McDowell, Dr. Richard G. Zweifel, and Mr. Russell Rak. To all of you, my deepest thanks. I alone claim responsibility for the contents as I've presented them. For his kindness and understanding, and without whom I might never have been introduced to natural history, I dedicate this work to my grandfather, the late Victor John Badaracco.

Introduction

In most dictionaries, and in the minds of most laymen, a lizard is a four-footed, scaly reptile with a long tail. In view of limbless species, short-tailed species, and the like, this definition falls somewhat short.

If we start at the class level, lizards are reptiles: poikilo-thermic (cold-blooded), scale covered, air breathing verte-brates. They can reproduce on land, and the young resemble the parents in form. They developed the amniote egg and a shell to retain moisture. The skull articulates with the atlas by one occipital condyle, and the mandible articulates with the cranium through the quadrate bone. The skin contains very few glands.

From here the lizards are further placed in the order Squa-mata, which they share with the snakes and dissimilar worm-lizards. These creatures share the following traits: cloacal open-ing transverse, male reproductive organ paired, Jacobson's or-gan usually well developed, and skull of the diapsid type.

The suborder Sauria (Lacertilia) comprises the lizards themselves. Unlike snakes, lizards possess the following charac-ters: mandibles firmly united anteriorly; eyelids, ear openings and limbs present in one or another combination; and lack of forked ribs. Snakes possess the zygosphenes and zygantra of the vertebra, while only some lizards (none legless) possess these.

The suborder Amphisbaenia was long placed as a family of the true lizards, but it has recently been placed as a distinct group within the Squamata (although this is not yet universally accepted). No members of this group have an external ear opening and the eyes lie concealed beneath the skin. Only one genus has limbs, and these consist solely of the front pair. The scales are arranged in ring-like rows, giving the overall appear-ance of a worm.

Greatly developed toe pads and very small scales are characteristic of most typical geckos. This is *Peropus mutilatus*. Photo by F.J. Dodd, Jr.

Goniocephalus grandis is one species of a genus of tree-dwelling agamids found in southern Asia and Australia. It is characterized by long thin legs and keeled scales. Photo by J. Bridges.

The Australian frilled dragon, *Chlamydosaurus kingii,* at rest and displaying the frill. Photos by G. Marcuse.

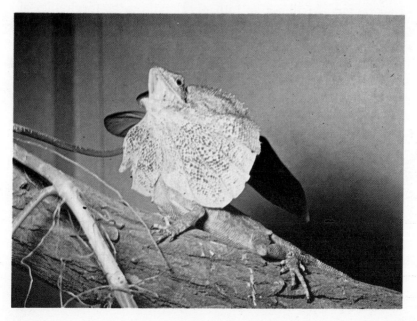

I have reduced a few families to subfamilial level in view of the recent work to simplify classification. I relegate the Gerrhosauridae to a subfamily of the Cordylidae, the Feyliniidae as a subfamily of the Scincidae, and the Anelytropsidae as a subfamily of the Dibamidae. The last arrangement, however, is only tentative and it may yet be proved that the two groups are distinct. I have given brief descriptions of the subfamilies of the Gekkonidae because certain references may still hold these groups at family level.

Detailed discussion about various species has been purposely avoided as the purpose of this book is a general compendium of facts about the classification, distribution, and adaptations within the suborder. Most matters of classification have been based on the works of earlier authors, notably Boulenger, Gadow, Worrell, and Bellairs. The items of cranial classification mentioned are based mainly on McDowell and Bogert and on Romer. Discussions of skull anatomy are based on these philosophies, which hopefully will be of some use to the layman in understanding the underlying methods of classification.

Color is not always a useful device in recognizing a species. This is because of color changes, geographic variability, and other factors. I will not go into any detail on the mechanics of color change, but instead advise the reader to see H.M. Smith's *Handbook of Lizards of the United States and Canada.*

Also, the topics of parthenogenesis and genetics have been ignored in this book as room is lacking for sufficient explanations. Those interested in this area would be advised to consult one of the journals listed in the bibliography.

Habitats

Lizards can be found in practically every habitat within their range, being absent only from the poles and the colder regions of the globe. Most abundant in the jungles and deserts of the lower latitudes, there do exist a few forms in cool climates, such as the European genus *Lacerta*. The Galapagos Islands harbor a marine lizard, while many parts of the world possess aquatic forms. There are many forms that are fossorial and rarely see the surface of their subterranean world. We will discuss each by habitat preference.

ARBOREAL

Whereas no reptile alive today can be considered aerial, we do come close with the Asian genus of "flying dragons,"

The flying gecko of Thailand, *Ptychozoon kuhli,* has skin folds on the tail, sides, and feet. Photo by the author.

Draco. The numerous species of the genus range throughout Indonesia, the Philippines, and the general area of Southeast Asia. The species have long flexible ribs which can expand like an umbrella, revealing a pair of large wings. They can use these

Agama agama, the rainbow lizard of northern Africa, is fairly easy to keep in captivity if given plenty of heat and some vegetable matter. Photo by Dr. O. Klee.

Tree lizards, *Calotes calotes,* are often called "bloodsuckers" because of their ability to turn bright red. Like the chameleons, the eyes can rotate independently of each other. Photo by H. Hansen, Aquarium Berlin.

to glide from tree to tree or to the ground. *Draco* have the ability, to some extent, to control their flight in regard to direction and climbing power.

Although not quite as elaborate, two gekkonid genera, *Ptychozoon* and *Mimetozoa*, also possess lateral flaps of skin. These lack the support of ribs, however, and act more as parachutes than gliders.

These genera are all tree dwellers and are remarkably adapted for such a way of life. But there are other traits an arboreal lizard can use to advantage, and we find the best example in the true chameleons of the Old World. These species possess a prehensile tail which acts as a fifth foot to grasp a branch and secure a good hold. This trait is not unique to chameleons, though. It is also found in the American alligator lizards (*Gerrhonotus*) and the Asian bark lizards (*Cophotis*).

Many other lizards are known to be tree climbers, including the giant monitors of the Varanidae. Some well known tree climbers are the two similar genera *Calotes* and *Japalura*. These are long-limbed agamids which feed on the insects that are found in trees. The American *Anolis* and *Iguana*, the Solomon Island *Corucia*, and geckos in general are all arboreal.

The habits may be as diverse as the species. On one extreme is the frail, quick *Draco*, while on the other is the bulky, slow *Chamaeleo*. The latter have become so physically slow that they have developed a long sticky (and quick) tongue to secure their prey. The eyes of this group move independently and give a special stereo view of the victim, increasing the accuracy of their aim.

AQUATIC

To date, only one living lizard is known to be marine. This is the Galapagos marine iguana, *Amblyrhynchus cristatus*. Found most often on the rocky shores of its island home, this lizard will forage in the ocean for its meal of seaweed. This lizard is not a very good swimmer, merely adequate. It can reduce its heartbeat and other bodily functions, probably as an aid in adjusting to the two environments in which it lives.

While *Amblyrhynchus* is unique in being marine, there exist many aquatic or semiaquatic lizards. One, *Shinisaurus crocodilurus*, is known to be a good swimmer and feeds on fish and molluscs from the streams of its home in southern China. *Shinisaurus* also climbs to some extent. It remains one of the rarest lizards in Western collections.

A much larger form is the agamid lizard *Hydrosaurus amboinensis*, a three- or four-foot long creature of the Pacific islands. This species sports a large dorsal and caudal crest and swims well. It is mainly herbivorous. In South America lives a genus of lizards, similar to but smaller than *Hydrosaurus*, known as basilisks (*Basiliscus*). These lizards are celebrated for their ability to run across the surface of a pond for several yards, bipedally, before sinking in.

South America also harbors many teiids, some of which are semiaquatic. The genus *Dracaena* is celebrated for its snail-crushing molars. The smaller *Crocodilurus* and *Neusticurus* are found near streams and ponds. The Bornean *Lanthanotus* is known to be fond of the water, while the true monitors have been seen swimming at sea miles from the nearest land.

TERRESTRIAL

By the term terrestrial is meant those forms most commonly found on the ground, under rocks, in deserts, etc. The only poisonous lizards belong to this group, as do many monitors, agamids, and iguanids. Some desert dwelling forms have developed fringes along the toes to give added traction in the loose sand. Many forms, such as the horned lizards (*Phrynosoma*), can burrow quickly into the sand, a device useful in escaping the rays of the sun. Many forms are bipedal and can run very rapidly. Others are nimble-footed around rocky areas and can easily lose themselves from view. The chuckwallas (*Sauromalus*) can secrete themselves inside a crevice then expand the lungs with air, making removal of the animal almost impossible. Many desert forms have horizontal bars beneath the tail. When pursued, the lizard curls the tail, revealing the bars. The resultant optical illusion makes the creature very difficult to follow.

Not all desert dwellers are diurnal. Some, such as certain geckos and the night lizards (Xantusiidae), are found roaming at night when all is cool. These little creatures rely on protec-

The only known marine lizard, *Amblyrhynchus cristatus,* the Galapagos marine iguana, often forms large herds on the shore. Because it eats sea plants, it is very difficult to keep in captivity; it is also legally protected. Photos by L. Flesher.

Leiocephalus carinatus, the small West Indian curly-tailed lizard. Photo by H. Hansen, Aquarium Berlin.

The Galapagos land iguana, *Conolophus subcristatus,* is the other large iguana restricted to the Galapagos. It is also protected. Photo by L. Flesher.

Since the common horned lizard requires live ants in captivity, it seldom lives for long. Its temperature and moisture requirements are also very strict. Photo by L. Van der Meid.

tive coloration and their small size for protection. They are able to secrete themselves into the very narrowest of crevices, and the only successful way of procuring them then is with a crowbar.

FOSSORIAL

To this group belong most of the limbless lizards. The creatures discussed here are those that live underground all or most of the time. Typically these lizards are specialized by having cylindrical bodies, pointed snouts, reduced eyes, and the external ear absent. The nostril is usually set horizontally, as opposed to facing upward in most lizards. The head shields are usually enlarged.

Those families whose members are fossorial are the Dibamidae, Anniellidae, some Scincidae, and some Pygopodidae. The earless monitor, *Lanthanotus*, may be fossorial or at least semifossorial. The genus *Dibamus* contains six diminutive species found in Southeast Asia. The largest may be eight inches long. The body is very thin, and the lizards of this group remain rare in collections because of their secretive habits. Also in this group is the Mexican *Anelytropsis papillosus*, a lizard which has only been collected about ten times. It is found in the desert, as opposed to the forests of Asia, and is probably wholly fossorial.

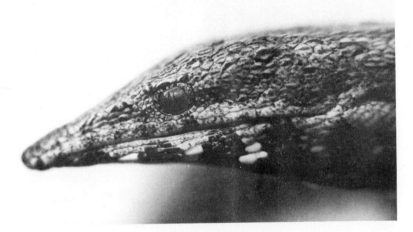

Burton's snake lizard, *Lialis burtonis*, does poorly in captivity. Photo by P. O'Brien, courtesy U. Kansas Mus. Nat. Hist.

The purely American Anniellidae, consisting of two species, is also mainly subterranean in habits. It is known to be found near moisture, in loose soil such as beaches. Unlike the Dibamidae, *Anniella* has functional eyes and well developed eyelids.

The Anguinidae have their share of burrowers, too, such as the well known slow-worm, *Anguis fragilis*, a worm-eating species found in Britain and continental Europe. They are remarkably long-lived for lizards, being kept in captivity for over 50 years, and are very effective eradicators of the garden slug.

Unique to Australia and New Guinea is a family known as "scaly-footed lizards," the Pygopodidae. They are characterized by being limbless save for a pair of flaps near the vent. They lack eyelids and the ear may be exposed or hidden. A further discussion of this family will be found under *Family Accounts*.

Two infrequently seen anoles. Above, *Anolis homolechis*; below, *Anolis roquet aeneus.* Photos by R.G. Tuck, Jr., courtesy U.S. National Mus.

Basiliscus basiliscus, a yard-long iguanid from Colombia and Central America, is capable of running over water. Young specimens were once commonly sold as pets. The crests are commonly sexually dimorphic in this genus, males having the larger crests. Photo by H. Hansen, Aquarium Berlin.

The Eurasian scheltopus, *Ophisaurus apodus,* is very closely related to the familiar American glass lizards. Photo by G. Marcuse.

In moving underground a lizard may employ one of several methods, the most common being a corkscrew-like use of the head and neck, literally pushing its way through the soil. In some, the head moves up and down while the body pushes the creature forward.

Crests and Ornamentation

With the popularity of science fiction being what it is today, few people have not seen a *Lost Island*-type picture where the bold scientist and his party encounter the "last surviving dinosaurs." One fact pervades all the grand attempts of the cinema to depict a dinosaur: all dinosaurs have to have crests, frills, or spines. The lizards and crocodilians used in these movies are always adorned with this fancy make-up.

But among the vast array of living lizards, few of the large ones possess such fancy accouterments, while many small forms are more bizarre than anything Hollywood could conceive. The large iguanas do have dorsal crests, but nothing like what one sees in the movies. Admittedly, there are a few large forms like *Hydrosaurus* which would fit the bill nicely, but they are exceptional.

Considered to be fairly plain lizards, the genus *Anolis* has members with a developed caudal sail, while males of the genus as a whole are known for their bright throat fans. The true chameleons have great diversity in facial horns, as do the agamid lizards of the genus *Harpesaurus*. *Ceratophora* has a single horn-like flap on the tip of its snout, while *Lyriocephalus* has a small globe on theirs.

The Australian lizard *Chlamydosaurus kingii* may have the most unique accessory of all. On either side of the body is a large flap of skin. When alarmed, the lizard extends these flaps even with the head, greatly enlarging its appearance. This trait has earned it the name of frilled dragon.

The list of bizarre forms goes on with the American horned lizards (*Phrynosoma*) and the Australian moloch (*Moloch*). There exists the beautiful union of form and function in the wings of *Draco*. Certain Central American teiids, genus *Proctoporus*, have light-reflecting spots along their sides; one form may even be bioluminescent.

Only a few iguanids are found outside the New World. Two which are rarely seen include *Oplurus grandidieri* (above) and *Oplurus cyclurus* (below). Photos courtesy U.S. National Mus.

A zebra-tailed lizard, *Callisaurus draconoides,* from the southwestern U.S. Photo by F.J. Dodd, Jr.

Corythophanes cristatus is representative of a small group of unusual iguanids. This specimen was taken in Honduras. Photo by J. Bridges.

Goniocephalus boydii, Boyd's forest dragon, from the rain forests of Queensland, Australia. Photo courtesy Australian Reptile Park.

The list of examples is a long one indeed, but what of function? It is known that the throat fans of some lizards are used to warn intruders infringing on a territory, as well as to attract a mate. The horns of male chameleons are used in territorial battles. The devices of many lizards are for protection, either by physical discomfort (the horns of *Phrynosoma*) or bluff (*Chlamydosaurus*). The dorsal sails of lizards like *Hydrosaurus* and *Basiliscus* are not fully explained. One idea is that this device is rich in blood vessels and helps to regulate internal temperature. To date, no one is quite sure.

Lizard Adaptations

Aside from the typical saurian characteristics mentioned in the introduction, there are certain distinguishing though non-universal traits found in lizards. The subject of this section will be the various modifications found in certain organs of the lizards.

The first structure to discuss is the lacertilian eye. The eye of a lizard may be extremely well developed with functional lids and color perception, or the eyes might be concealed under a layer of skin, making them useless. The pupil could be elliptical or round. In the Gekkonidae, at least, many forms possess compound eyeballs. In the Chamaeleontidae the eyes are

The eyes of a gecko have several openings to help concentrate light. Photo by R. Pawley.

covered by a thick membrane of skin with a small aperture near the middle. Each eyeball can move independently of the other, a trait not wholly confined to the chameleons but found in a few other lizard genera as well (i.e., *Calotes*).

The leopard lizard, *Gambelia wislizenii*, is an active southwestern U.S. species that does fairly well in captivity. It was formerly placed in the genus *Crotaphytus*. Photo by J.K. Langhammer.

The spiny horned lizards of the southwestern U.S. (such as this *Phrynosoma cornutum*) bear a startling resemblance to the unrelated Australian thorny devil. Photo by J.K. Langhammer.

Chamaeleo melleri is a large species from eastern Africa. Often the shape of the rostral appendages or nose horns (if present) can be used to identify chameleons, as can the shape of crests behind the head. Photo by H. Hansen, Aquarium Berlin.

The pupil itself is usually a clue to the habits of the lizard, in that vertical pupils are common to nocturnal forms while round pupils are common to diurnal species. As in any pupil, the aperture is widest in darkness and may be nearly as large as the eye, as in many geckos. In bright light the pupil contracts, becoming a small opening.

It is known that many lizards possess the ocular cones needed for color vision. This is useful in determining breeding colors and territorial warnings.

The lower lid of the lizard is usually the most developed lid. It may contain a clear spectacle or window so the lizard can see with its eyes closed. Many geckos, the Pygopodidae, and certain other groups lack movable eyelids. Instead, the eye is covered by a clear rounded scale, keeping the eye permanently open. To clean this scale lidless lizards can utilize the tongue.

The ear of a lizard can be either exposed or concealed. In some species the tympanic cavity is covered by a clear thin membrane. The Chamaeleontidae, Lanthanotidae, Dibamidae, and Anniellidae all lack an external ear opening. Many skinks, some agamids, and a variety of other species also lack the external ear. Hearing, however, is not dependent solely upon airborne sounds, but can be detected by an acute sense of feel, especially in blind, earless forms.

Another feature associated with the head is the tongue. The long forked and protrusible tongue is common to the Varanidae, the teiid *Tupinambis*, and a few smaller forms. Many lizards have the anterior portion of the tongue nicked, but not all have retractable tongues. The most interesting tongue is that of the chameleon. It is a projectable affair with a sticky tip and may be as long as the body of the lizard itself. When employed it is fired quickly, and accurately, to secure the insect prey. Most lizards use the tongue as an organ to bring particles of air to the Jacobson's organ, while others use it only mechanically as an aid to swallowing.

As far as limbs go, we can generalize by saying that many burrowing forms are limbless or have reduced legs, and most arboreal lizards have long limbs with long digits. Limbs are of little use to fossorial lizards. One or both pairs of legs may be absent, and the number of claws could be less than five. In the

A female *Chamaeleo cristatus*. Notice the unusual form of the eye and feet. Photo by Dr. O. Klee.

Unlike snakes, which shed the skin in one piece, many lizards shed in patches. Reptiles exhibit their brightest patterns just after shedding.

Close-up of the toe pads of a gecko. Each ridge or lamella contains millions of microscopic hooks which give the lizard incredible traction. Photo by G. Marcuse.

swift desert species where bipedality is common, the hind limbs may be quite strong and longer than the forelimbs. In species that can leap well, as in the American collared lizards (*Crotaphytus*), this situation is readily apparent. Those lizards not so swift of foot, such as horned lizards and Gila monsters, are equipped with strong nearly equal-sized limbs, usually with strong claws.

In regard to limbs, the geckos and certain *Anolis* have developed a special toe pad composed of millions of microscopic hooks which give the lizard the ability to scale most objects and to even walk along ceilings. While this feature is not universal among geckos, it is a trait by which most geckos are known.

The tail of many lizards is known as an excellent defense from predators because it can often be disconnected from the rest of the body. Being broken at a special point on the tail vertebra, the muscles and blood vessels contract and the tail is lost. The contraction of blood vessels allows almost no bleeding. In those lizards that rely heavily on this defense, the tail will eventually regenerate. This process of tail or limb loss is known as *autotomy*. The regrown tail will not be as long nor as perfect as the original, nor will it contain any true vertebrae.

The tail has other purposes in other species. We already described the prehensile tail. In those forms that run bipedally, the tail is a necessary organ of balance. Species that need this organ for balance, such as *Crotaphytus* and *Chlamydosaurus*, do not readily lose the tail.

Certain lizards have relatively short tails, with a special purpose. The Old World agamids *Uromastix* and *Agama batillifera* have tails shorter than the head and body length, but these tails are equipped with sharp spines, a defense against potential predators. If they must secure themselves in a crevice, they keep the tail facing the entrance to discourage pursuit.

The Gila monster and beaded lizard both have bulky tails. This organ serves as a fat reserve from which the lizards can derive nourishment during times of bad hunting.

Dangerous Lizards

While it is true that any lizard caught by hand is likely to bite, only a very few are likely to cause any real harm. Certain large lizards, those over two feet long, may bite hard enough to draw blood, but only two species are venomous out of the numerous species of known lizards. These are the Gila monster and the beaded lizard (*Heloderma suspectum* and *H. horridum*, respectively) of the southwestern United States and western Mexico. Both are thick bodied, blunt headed, and stout tailed. All but one subspecies are mottled orange or yellow and black; the other form, from lower Mexico, is solid black. The

The only venomous lizard in the United States, the Gila monster (*Heloderma suspectum*) is now protected by law in the few areas it occurs. Photo by G. Marcuse.

Detail of the head of the Gila monster. Notice the non-overlapping scales and swollen lower jaw. From Van Denburgh.

name beaded lizard is a good one, for the non-overlapping scales resemble Indian bead work. The eyes are small and lidded; the ear is externally visible. The tongue is dark and frequently flicked like that of a snake.

The cheek area of these species will appear swollen, as it is here that the poison glands lie. Unlike snakes, the injection mechanism is located in the lower jaw. The poison flows into the lizard's mouth and seeps into the wound caused by the long teeth. Although the teeth are grooved, they do not effectively conduct the venom flow. Because the actual injection of venom is uncertain, the lizard must hold on to the victim to increase the possibility of injection, instead of simply striking like most poisonous snakes.

While these lizards are generally believed to be slow and lethargic, a *Heloderma* can turn quite rapidly and secure a good hold on anyone foolish enough to disturb one.

Although not venomous, there are certain other lizards that can be a lot to reckon with if disturbed. The monitor lizards, genus *Varanus*, include the largest living lizards. The true giants, such as the Komodo dragon, Perentie, or water monitor, could easily dispatch a man. The teeth, claws, and weight of these lizards would make them a formidable bunch of adversaries. Indeed some, like the Komodo dragon, rule supreme in their native haunts.

While not overtly aggressive, even the moderately large monitors will turn on a potential threat. The smaller species of *Varanus*, as well as *Tupinambis* and *Dracaena*, could cause severe wounds and are reportedly capable of removing a finger. While not poisonous as such, a bite from one of these creatures could be quite serious.

The large size and bad temper of the Komodo dragon make it unsuitable for handling, even if it were still legal to own them. Photo by Dr. O. Klee.

A tegu, *Tupinambis teguixin,* eating a rat. The bite of this species and other large lizards is painful, although not venomous, and could cause serious wounds. Photo by G. Marcuse.

In captivity all the lizards I've mentioned can become docile and freely allow handling. If exposed to sunlight, however, a strange transformation takes place. The animal slowly regains its more aggressive instincts and may become vicious if an attempt is made to handle it. It has been reported by Ditmars that large monitors may charge and attack their regular keeper. The lizards inflate their lungs, give off ominous hissing noises, and lash at their victim with the long tail. The tail of a monitor can break the legs of a dog; a large one could probably knock over a man.

Basic Anatomy

In this section I have tried to outline the more important elements used in establishing a system of effective classification and at the same time to enlighten the layman to the "little things" that are a very important part of making a lizard a lizard. Although this chapter is brief, it is as complete as space allows and as accurate as possible.

SKULL

In general discussions about the head of an animal, the upper portion is referred to as the *cranium*, while the lower part consists of the *mandible*. In lizards the foremost bone of the mandible is the dentary; it is at the foremost point of the dentary bone that the two halves of the mandibles are firmly united (the symphysis). The mandible articulates with the cranium at the quadrate bone, located near the rear of the cranium. The coronoid bone juts up behind the dentary bone and fits into a socket formed by the pterygoid bones of the cranium. The distance from the tip of the snout to the coronoid intersection determines the gape of the lizard.

In the mandible, teeth are found on the dentary bone; in the cranium they may be on the maxillary, premaxillary, palatine, or pterygoid bones. The teeth themselves may be pleurodont (along the side of the bone) or acrodont (along the crest of the bone). In some lizards thecodont teeth (fitting into sockets) are found, but along with one of the other types. The teeth may be pyramidal, conical, flat, bicuspid, or tricuspid. They can be quickly and frequently replaced.

Between the maxillary, premaxillary, and septomaxillary bones is a large gap in the cranium. This is in effect the internal nasal arch through which the nostrils draw air through the skull into the mouth. Another gap exists a little behind this,

Skull of a lizard with major bones indicated.

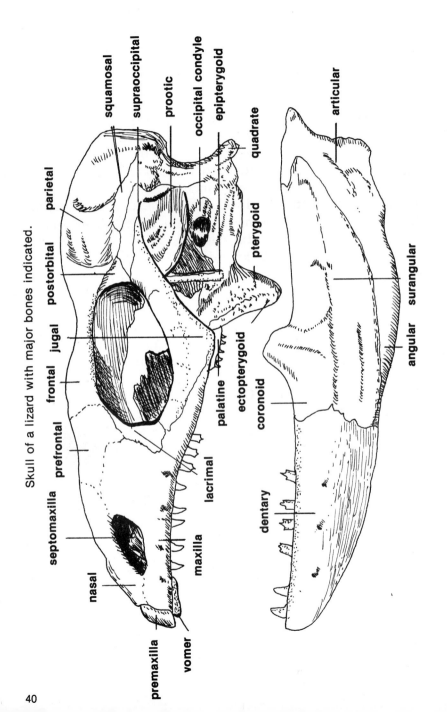

usually near the middle of the skull, and it is here that the eye is housed. Above the ocular cavity is a bone or pair of bones called the frontals. This is a centrally located bone met anteriorly by the nasals or occasionally the prefrontal. It is bordered posteriorly by the parietal. Along the border of the frontal and parietal, or often in the center of the parietal, may be found a single round hole. It is in this small aperture that the pineal gland or third eye is located. In species lacking the eye, this pineal foramen is often absent.

There may be a temporal arch, an arch of bone created by the postorbital and squamosal bones. The lower arch, formed by an extension of the jugal with the quadrate, is not found in lizards, but does occur in the tuatara, *Sphenodon*, a lizard-like animal of New Zealand. In some lizards and all snakes the upper temporal arch is lacking; in these forms the squamosal bone is rudimentary or absent.

One last aspect of the skull that should be mentioned is the occipital condyle, the point where the cranium is fixed to the skull. This is a point of bone (single in lizards and the other reptiles) where the first vertebra, the atlas, attaches to the skull. It is not always at the hindmost part of the skull.

POSTCRANIAL SKELETON

The vertebrae are the first bones encountered beyond the skull. The first vertebra is the atlas, so named because it must bear the skull. The second bone is the axis, the pivot point which allows free movement of the head and neck. The hyoid apparatus is in the throat, roughly beneath and in front of these first vertebrae. It may be connected with a vertebra, or it may be a free unit. It protects the windpipe.

The body of the vertebra is called a centrum; the space between centra is the intercentrum. The vertebral centra may be one of two types, either amphicoelous (biconcave) or procoelus (concave anteriorly, convex posteriorly). The backbone runs the entire length of the tail, but should this member be lost, the replacement will be forever devoid of true vertebrae. Along the tail section, when true vertebrae are present, one can locate the plane of autotomy, which is usually a cartilaginous plate before or behind the transverse process of the vertebra.

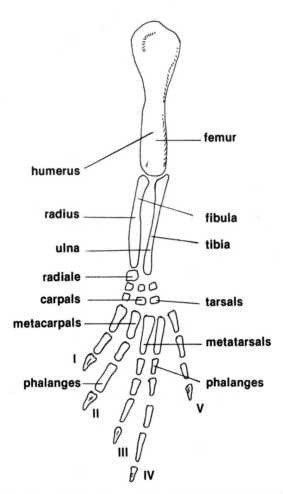

Generalized lizard limb. Bones of foreleg on left, those of hind leg on right.

The forelimbs are supported from the pectoral girdle. The humerus bone articulates at a point between the sternum and interscapula. Similarly, the femur fits into an opening of the ischium. At the lowest point of the pectoral girdle is the sternum, a bone which protects a good part of the internal organs. Between the sternum and the pelvis may be a bony or cartilaginous union of the ribs, known as the parasternum. Extending from beneath the scapula and uniting with the sternum is the clavicle, a bone always present in pairs.

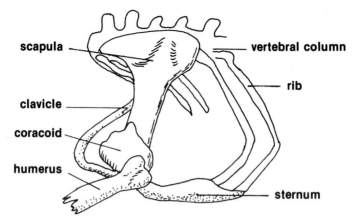

scapula — — vertebral column

— rib

clavicle —

coracoid —

humerus —

— sternum

Lizard pectoral girdle,
anterior end at left.

EAR

The ear is an important organ for balance as well as hearing. Sound waves hitting the tympanic membrane are relayed by the bone structure to an auditory nerve where the impulse is received and transmitted to the brain for analysis. Even in "earless" lizards there is some internal structure, although sound might be detected by certain jaw bones.

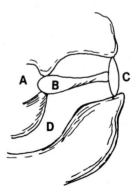

Cross-section of lizard ear. A: inner
ear cavity; B: stapes; C: tympanic
membrane; D: eustachian tube.

BRAIN

While it is a well known fact that the brain of a huge dinosaur was scarcely the size of a walnut, the brains of modern reptiles are small and simple in structure, though they are proportionately larger. There are three major areas, designated the cerebral hemispheres, the midbrain, and the cerebellum. Anterior to the cerebral hemisphere is a stalk of variable length and thickness known as the olfactory bulb. This is the principal scent detector and varies in size depending üpon the capabilities of scent detection among species. Beneath the cerebral hemispheres is a small stalk containing the pituitary gland (growth and development) and the thalamus and hypothalamus (activity and homeostatic controls). This central stalk as a whole is called the diencephalon.

Behind the cerebral hemispheres is the midbrain. This may also be referred to as the optic lobe, as it is here that the message from the eye is translated. If present, the pineal eye may still have the nerve that connects with the midbrain.

Next come the cerebellum and medulla. The medulla is the start of the spinal cord. It regulates heartbeat and respiration, and it is to this area that the messages for balance are sent from the ear.

HEART

The saurian heart is a three chambered pump. It consists of a right and left auricle and a large ventrical chamber.

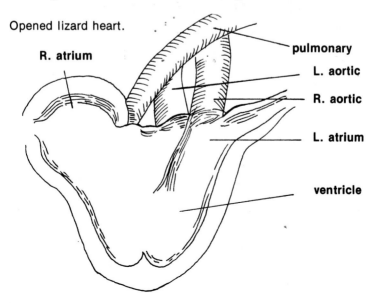

Opened lizard heart.

R. atrium

pulmonary

L. aortic

R. aortic

L. atrium

ventricle

JACOBSON'S ORGAN

This celebrated feature is probably better developed in snakes than lizards. It is a system of nerves entering a cavity in the roof of the mouth. When air particles are collected with the tongue, the lizard places the tongue against this organ for analysis.

SKIN

The epidermal coat of lizards is a scaly layer, the scales usually overlapping. Because the animals are poikilothermic and because they need not be kept moist, the skin is remarkably devoid of glands. In some species there may be a fine coat of bead-like bony pieces beneath the skin. These are called osteoderms. They may be fused to the bones of the head, making the skin immovable.

The heavy scales of the sungazer, *Cordylus giganteus,* are adequate protection against most predators. Photo by G. Marcuse.

The scales themselves may be smooth or keeled. If they are smooth, they will feel like fine leather and very often appear polished. If they are keeled, they may be rough or spiny, depending on the species.

Lizards in Captivity

There is no question that the keeping of lizards for pets is an increasingly popular hobby in our time. Many thousands of specimens will be purchased, and a great many will die due to improper care. It must be realized that many lizards cannot be kept alive in captivity at this time because of their delicate nature or specialized diets. The methods that are described in this section are aimed at caring for the more adaptable species.

In selecting a cage suitable for housing lizards it should be remembered that these are usually active creatures which could injure themselves by rubbing against screen or wire. The best item to use in constructing a cage would be glass. Large aquariums make excellent quarters. They should be provided with a close-fitting top and a warm light source.

The floor of the cage can be covered with almost any kind of stratum, dependent mainly upon the needs of the species kept. At the bottom of the cage should be placed a layer of newspaper or cardboard upon which the soil is placed, making it easier to remove the soil when necessary. Sometimes a layer of charcoal is placed beneath the soil to act something like a filter system, helping to keep the soil from becoming too moist.

A light source that will provide some amount of heat is a must, especially in the cooler months. During the warmer part of the year the terrarium may be placed in a location where it will receive natural sunlight. However, a suitable amount of shade must be provided, lest the "cold-blooded" inhabitants absorb too much heat and die. Objects used to provide cool retreats may consist of rocks, bark, small logs, plants, etc.

Since many species like to climb, notably the geckos and some iguanids, perches must be provided. In the case of small lizards, potted plants, twigs, and the like will suffice, while the larger forms need stouter branches or shelves which can bear their weight.

In American petshops the common anole, *Anolis carolinensis*, is still the most frequently seen reptile. Photo by A. van Raam.

As in aquarium keeping, terrarists should not overcrowd a cage with too many individuals. The sizes of the specimens should be similar, as even a large herbivore could kill a smaller lizard by trampling it to death. Care must be taken to assure that one species is not predatory upon the others, lest the collection eventually merge into one well supplied stomach!

In supplying a diet for a collection of lizards, it must be remembered that variety is important for any species if at all possible. While mealworms make a convenient food for most lizards, a diet consisting solely of this foodstuff can result in stomach troubles and may kill the lizard. A sick lizard should never be offered such an item; lizards do not chew their food, but swallow it whole (at least small insects), and a sick lizard may lack the strength of jaws to crush the mealworm before swallowing. Many a specimen has been found dead with a mealworm boring its way out of the animal's body because it was not killed. Aside from that, an overabundance of chitin, the hard coat of an insect, may block the digestive tract.

Such animals as tegus, monitors, and beaded lizards will readily consume a dish of beaten eggs. To provide variety, chopped meat, fish, and bonemeal should be mixed in occasionally.

A good assortment for insectivorous lizards should include hard and soft beetles, crickets, earthworms, moths, and slugs. Beetles with very colorful shiny shells seem particularly attractive; I have seen small ground skinks, *Lygosoma laterale*, attempt to attack the Japanese beetle, an impossible task because of the beetle's large size. Some species, such as the moloch, flying dragons, and horned lizards, have an almost exclusive diet of ants or termites. Getting these is usually no problem, but those the lizards do not eat have a nasty habit of escaping through the air holes of the cage! Larger species of carnivores may take mice, fish, other lizards, snakes, or similar prey.

Although mealworms are good food for some lizards, their hard body can cause digestive problems. Photo by L. Van der Meid.

The plant-eating forms are easier to supply with food. The common green iguana is fond of lettuce, berries, and fruit cocktail. Many forms will take yellow dandelion flowers, tomatoes, bananas, and most other vegetable items. Surprisingly, I find that my plant-eating beasts prefer the leaves of our mulberry trees to most other items, including the berries. The herbivores are a delicate lot, and I find that many will not eat except at rather high temperatures, around 100 degrees F. Examples include the spiny-tailed agamas, *Uromastix*, as well as the American *Dipsosaurus* and *Sauromalus*.

In providing water, one should bear in mind that many species will not accept liquid from a dish. Therefore the cage must periodically be sprinkled to simulate dew or rain.

FAMILY ACCOUNTS

Leaf-tailed gecko, *Phyllurus cornutus*, from eastern Australia. Photo courtesy Australian Reptile Park.

Gekkonidae

All geckos have four limbs, each with five digits. The tongue is flat. Postorbital and squamosal arches are absent. The skin is soft and loose, and the scales are generally granular and non-overlapping. The following subfamilies were often considered full families in older literature:

Subfamily Gekkoninae: Vertebrae amphicoelous, parietals distinct, eyelids absent, nasal bones distinct.

Subfamily Eublepharidae: Vertebrae procoelous, parietal single, movable eyelids present.

Subfamily Uroplatinae: As Gekkoninae, but nasal bones united.

Gekko gecko sounding off. Only geckos among the lizards have real voices. Photo by R. Pawley.

The leopard gecko, *Eublepharis macularis,* of Asia has functional eyelids and lacks toe pads. It is mistakenly considered to be poisonous by
natives of its homeland. Photo by H. Hansen, Aquarium Berlin.

Phyllodactylus marmorata, the marbled gecko, is a widespread Australian species that grows to nearly six inches in length. Photo courtesy Australian Reptile Park.

Above: *Oedura marmorata*, the velvet gecko of Australia. **Below:** *Diplodactylus* species, an Australian gecko with retractile claws. Photos courtesy Australian Reptile Park.

53

This family lacks large head shields and is the only saurian group with vocal sacs, giving the geckos a true voice. The lizards of this group are normally arboreal and nocturnal. Color in the geckos may be somber, as in *Hemidactylus turcicus*, or extraordinarily bright, as in the Madagascan *Phelsuma*.

These lizards lack any true giants. The tokay (*Gekko gecko*) may reach a foot in length, while *Sphaerodactylus elasmorhynchus* is barely an inch long, smaller than its printed name.

The Gekkonidae is noted for the variety of tail structure. Many forms have carrot- or turnip-shaped tails. *Phyllurus* of Australia has a tail resembling a second head. *Uroplates* and *Ptychozoon* have a membrane of skin surrounding the tail. The American banded geckos, genus *Coleonyx*, may wave the tail above the body when disturbed, as would a cat.

This family is extremely large and very widespread throughout the warmer regions of the world. They have increased their range by being transported inadvertently with fruit shipments or by rafting from one island to another, a successful device in the Caribbean. In many cases these lizards exist in human dwellings. In some parts of Asia there is a belief that a gecko's cry during the birth of a child is a sign of good fortune. The group as a whole is very useful in controlling insect pests.

Most geckos are oviparous, but some New Zealand species give birth to living young.

Most geckos make excellent pets and will thrive if properly cared for. The only drawback to most hobbyists is the nocturnal habits of most of the species.

Pygopodidae

Postorbital and squamosal arches absent. Prefrontal and postfrontal bones in contact. Pterygoids toothless. Forelimbs absent, the hind pair being represented by vestigial flaps. Eyelids absent. Ear concealed or exposed. Large shields on head. Traces of vocal sacs sometimes present. Wholly confined to Australia and New Guinea.

The majority of these creatures are secretive, living in rocky areas, in high grass, or in burrows. Some can move about freely on the tops of the long wild grasses of their habitat. None are aquatic or arboreal. Some will be found active by day, while many of the desert forms are crepuscular or nocturnal wanderers.

Because they lack movable eyelids, the eye is always open as in snakes and bears a remarkable resemblance to the gekkonid eye. The tongue is long and flat and is used to clean the

Head of *Pygopus lepidopodus,* the common scaly-foot. Like the geckos, the eyes lack eyelids, but the pupil is round, not slit-like. Photo by P. O'Brien, courtesy U. Kansas Mus. Nat. Hist.

Dorsal view of the head of *Lialis burtonis*. Photo by P. O'Brien, courtesy U. Kansas Mus. Nat. Hist.

ocular spectacle. Because of the lidless eye and the fact that many forms lack an external ear, it is necessary to use certain other traits to differentiate pygopodids from snakes. The tail of these lizards is longer than the head and body length, while in snakes it is shorter. The pygopodids have flap-like hind limbs, while snakes are devoid of anything like them. Some of these lizards have preanal pores, organs absent in snakes, and the tongue of a pygopodid is flat and broad, unlike the tongue of their ophidian counterparts. Lastly, the ventral scales of snakes are never divided into two rows as they are in this family.

The Pygopodidae has been somewhat neglected in popular herpetological literature, but among their numbers are some extraordinarily rare lizards. Discovered in 1897, *Ophidiocephalus taeniatus* remains known by only the single type specimen. A strange beast is this, for the ventral surface is darker than the dorsal. It was described as being found in central Australia.

Another rarity is the eight-inch long *Pletholax gracilis*, again known from a paucity of specimens. It is found in southwestern Australia.

There are currently eight recognized genera and fourteen species and subspecies. All are insectivorous, but the family giant, *Lialis burtonis*, will consume small lizards and snakes. This form may be three feet long, while most other species are under eighteen inches in length. The more commonly seen forms include *Lialis*, the four *Pygopus* species, and the tiny *Aprasia*. While very little is known of the natural history of these lizards, most of them are known to be oviparous, and the other species probably are, too.

Agamidae

Arches present. Four limbs present, pentadactyl except in *Sitana*, which is tetradactyl. Eyelids present. Osteoderms absent. Premaxillary single. Tail not autotomic. Dentition acrodont. Oviparous or viviparous.

This is a large family confined to the Old World. They are absent from Madagascar, where their New World counterparts, the Iguanidae, occur. Agamids are a diverse group including such extremes as the flying dragons and *Hydrosaurus*. *Hydrosaurus* is the giant of the family, growing to over three feet in length, but most species are about a foot or so long. Most species are oviparous, but a few, notably the Asian *Cophotis*, give birth to live young. Most species are insectivorous. Some larger forms will take smaller vertebrates, while a good many are herbivorous.

Calotes calotes, the bloodsucker. Photo by Muller Schmida.

Left: Displaying bearded dragon, *Amphibolurus barbatus.* Photo by Muller Schmida. **Below:** Young rainforest dragon, *Goniocephalus spinipes.* Photo courtesy Australian Reptile Park.

The extremely spiny scales are good defensive structures for the bearded dragon, *Amphibolurus barbatus*, of Australia. Photo courtesy Australian Reptile Park.

The common *Agama agama* is representative of the largely African genus with many species. Photo by Dr. O. Klee.

The large frill or ruff of *Chlamydosaurus kingii* is one of the most sensational defensive developments in the lizards. Photo courtesy Australian Reptile Park.

Eastern waterdragons, *Physignathus lesueurii,* from Australia. The genus extends as far west as India and includes a small assemblage of large tree-dwellers. Photo above courtesy Australian Reptile Park, that below by G. Marcuse.

The fearsome-looking thorny devil or moloch, *Moloch horridus*, is in reality a seven- to twelve-inch ant eater. The large thorns on the neck probably divert attention from the head. Photo courtesy Australian Reptile Park.

Two African spiny-tailed agamids: above, *Uromastix acanthurus;* below, *Uromastix hardwicki.* These are desert species requiring a rich vegetable diet and temperatures in excess of 100° F.

Chamaeleo chamaeleon, a slow-moving master of disguise, ranges north to Europe. Photo by Knaack.

The desert night lizard, *Xantusia vigilis,* is a member of a strictly New World family of uncertain relationships; they show features of the geckos, teiids, skinks, and anguids. Photo by F.J. Dodd, Jr.

Leiolepis belliana, the butterfly lizard of southern Asia, digs long deep tunnels. It has high heat requirements and needs a varied diet. The orange sides can be extended like *Draco*. Photo by Muller Schmida.

Australia is home to the large agamid genus *Amphibolurus*, which includes some well known species such as the bearded dragon (*A. barbatus*), the defenseless dragon (*A. reticulatus*), and the jacky lizard (*A. muricatus*). The rare *Chelosania brunnei* is endemic to the Island Continent, as are the Tommy round heads (*Diporiphora*) and the earless dragons (*Tympanocryptis*).

The various tree-dwelling genera *Calotes, Japalura, Lyriocephalus, Lophocalotes, Dendragama*, and *Harpesaurus* are all agamids, as are the desert-dwelling *Phrynocephalus* and *Moloch* and the many forest species of *Chlamydosaurus* and *Agama*. The continent of Africa is the headquarters of the genus *Agama*, a large group including some very colorful species. Africa also hosts many of the *Uromastix* species.

Iguanidae

These lizards are the New World's answer to the Agamidae, differing mainly by having pleurodont dentition. All are four-limbed and pentadactyl. They occur to a limited extent in the Old World in Madagascar, Fiji, and a few Pacific islands.

The giant of this family is a true giant among lizards. Growing to six feet long, this is the green iguana (*Iguana iguana*) so well known to terrarium keepers. The various other species in the many other genera of iguanas, such as *Cyclura*, *Amblyrhynchus*, and *Conolophus*, are all predominantly herbivorous, while most of the smaller forms are carnivores. Even in the United States, which lacks any giant iguanids, the larger

An adult *Iguana iguana*.
Photo by Muller
Schmida.

Lacerta muralis brueggemanni, a European wall lizard. Photo by H. Hansen, Aquarium Berlin.

Eremias nitida, a small African lacertid. Photo by J.T. Collins.

The common European green lizard, *Lacerta viridis*. The lacertids closely parallel the New World teiids. The differences cannot always be seen externally; all lacertids have four limbs and pleurodont teeth. Photo by H. Hansen, Aquarium Berlin.

The desert iguana, *Dipsosaurus dorsalis* (above), and the chuckwalla, *Sauromalus obesus* (below), two large heat-loving herbivores of the American West. Photos by L. Van der Meid.

Leiocephalus cubensis (right) and *Leiocephalus carinatus* (below) are two common Caribbean iguanids. Photos by G. Marcuse.

Tegus are large popular lizards requiring a varied diet and plenty of room. Above is the red tegu, *Tupinambis rufescens*. Photo by H. Hansen, Aquarium Berlin.

Ameiva ameiva, the common ameiva, is a teiid frequently sold as a "rainbow lizard." Photo by Dr. Herbert R. Axelrod.

Cordylus warreni, a commonly imported armadillo lizard or zonure. This genus produces living young. Photo by G. Marcuse.

The eastern fence lizard, *Sceloporus undulatus,* is a common species of spiny American iguanids. Photo by Muller Schmida.

species of *Sauromalus* and *Dipsosaurus* are plant eaters, as opposed to the smaller insect-eating *Phrynosoma* and *Anolis.*

One of the largest of the lizard genera belongs in this family. *Anolis* comprises at least three hundred species, most no more than a foot in length. They are most widely distributed in the Caribbean and South America and are generally arboreal. A few forms, such as *Anolis allogus* and *A. aquaticus,* are found on rocks near streams, into which they dive at the first sign of danger. The members of this genus are sometimes called chameleons, a name rightfully belonging to an African family only distantly related. Nevertheless, many of these species, and a good many lizards of other genera, have to a small extent the ability to change colors. To this genus, too, belong a good many species with gecko-like toe pads allowing very interesting acrobatic feats.

*Basiliscus
basiliscus.*
Photo by
Muller Schmida.

Ctenosaura is a small group of very similar land iguanas from Mexico and Central America. Photo by G. Marcuse.

Cordylus cordylus, an armadillo lizard from southern Africa. These bizarrely scaled lizards make popular pets. Photo by G. Marcuse.

Platysaurus sp., a close relative of *Cordylus* but lacking the impressive body armament. Photo by H. Hansen, Aquarium Berlin.

Detail of the head of *Cordylus giganteus.* Photo by G. Marcuse.

Tropidurus semitaeniatus, a South American iguanid related to the lava lizards of the Galapagos. Photo by G. Marcuse.

Among the iguanids are found the spiny lizards (*Sceloporus*), the lava lizards (*Tropidurus*), and the bipedal-running collared and leopard lizards (*Crotaphytus* and *Gambelia*, respectively) and basilisks (*Basiliscus*). While many of the iguanids, especially the North American forms, have been dealt with quite thoroughly, there are still species about which little is known. However, with the recent upsurge of interest in the zoology of South America, even obscure genera such as *Aptycholaemus* and *Deiroptyx* will soon be better known.

One note of interest to students of zoogeography is the pair of Madagascan genera. Occurring in what should be Agamidae territory, the genera *Oplurus* and *Chalarodon* resemble strongly those lizards inhabiting the New World. Exactly what they are doing in Madagascar is an interesting problem.

Chamaeleontidae

A purely Old World group centered in Africa, Madagascar, and southern Asia. They are recognized by their unusual eyes, casque-like heads, laterally compressed bodies, and opposing toes. The tongue is long and projectable; the tail is prehensile. The ear is concealed. At least one species ranges into parts of Europe. Most lay eggs.

Chamaeleo jacksoni, the familiar but ever-impressive three-horned chameleon. Photo by G. Marcuse.

The gigantic genus *Eumeces* comprises many very similar skinks. Shown here is the African species *Eumeces schneideri*. Photo by H. Hansen, Aquarium Berlin.

Chalcides sepsoides is a specialized burrowing skink. Notice the reduced legs and cylindrical shape. Photo by Dr. W. Bohme.

The red ground skink, *Lygosoma fernandi,* a large desert skink from Algeria. Photo by J.K. Langhammer.

Egernia cumminghami is one of several Australian skinks which have keeled scales instead of the usual glossy surface. Photo by Dr. O. Klee.

Although chameleons do not make good pets because of their short life in captivity and their slow movements, their unusual form and habits will continue to make them popular with hobbyists. This is *Chamaeleo cristatus*. Photo by Dr. O. Klee.

Microsaura pumila, a dwarf chameleon. Adult at right, young below. Photos by Muller Schmida.

Although venomous, the Gila monster, *Heloderma suspectum,* becomes tame in captivity. It will sit for hours in a shallow dish of water. Photo by H. Hansen, Aquarium Berlin.

Lanthanotus borneensis, the earless monitor. This very rare lizard is not a monitor and has (internal) ears. Photo by J.T. Collins.

Gould's goanna, *Varanus gouldii,* is an Australian monitor nearly five feet long. Monitor identification depends greatly on features of the nostril and tail. Photo by Dr. O. Klee.

This remarkable clan of saurians is most celebrated for their ability to change color. Despite popular belief, they cannot assume the designs of a plaid or checkerboard. Color is not always a function of camouflage, but is a result of mood, light, and temperature. In some chameleons the range of colors assumed is diverse, while in others it consists of changing from one shade of color to another.

The longest chameleon may be a yard long, and a few others reach nearly this size. Most species of the genus *Chamaeleo* are at least a foot or more in length, but the related genera are typically small and include some of the smallest living lizards.

These are slow-moving arboreal creatures that rely on keen sight and careful stalking to secure their prey. Upon sighting an insect, a chameleon will move toward the target so slowly that the eye can barely follow it. If there is a breeze, the lizard will gently rock back and forth. With the flattened body, the result looks like a leaf fluttering in the wind. Once within range of the insect, the lizard quickly releases the long sticky tongue and the insect becomes a meal.

While the European slow-worm may live for fifty years in captivity, few chameleons have passed the three-year mark. Most perish in the first six months. Exactly what factor is present or absent in captive conditions is unknown; indeed, it could just be that these lizards have an extremely short life span (though this is unlikely for the larger species). Little field work has been done to determine the natural life, so for now we just don't know. Nevertheless, chameleons are often kept as pets and will feed on a variety of insect matter and drink plenty of water, until they suddenly cease to live.

The little lizards of the genera *Brookesia* and *Microsaura* constitute the rest of the family. *Microsaura* is probably the largest in size of the two and gives birth to live young. The small chameleons formerly placed in *Rhampholeon* have considerably smaller tails than their allies, but their habits are similar.

Xantusiidae

A strictly American family, found in the United States, Cuba, Mexico, and parts of South America. There are four currently accepted genera, all being similar to geckos in having soft skin with small scales, lacking eyelids, and having a flat tongue. They lack toe pads and vocal sacs, however, and possess head shields and ventral plates. The genus *Xantusia* is viviparous.

The genus *Cricosaura* is monotypic (*C. typica*), inhabiting Cuba and possibly some of the nearby islands. It is probably the smallest member of the family.

The night lizard *Xantusia vigilis* is associated with Joshua trees in the Mohave desert. From Van Denburgh.

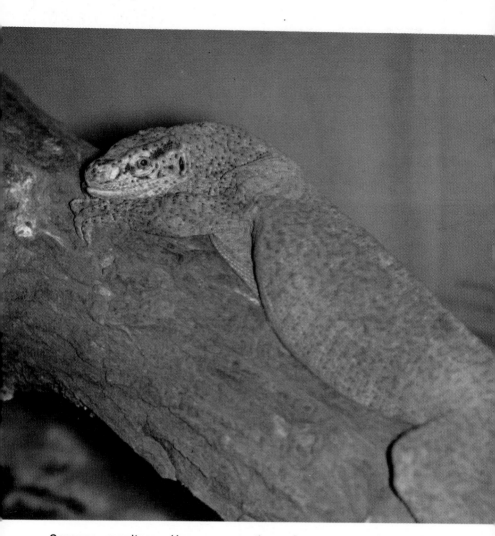

Savanna monitors, *Varanus exanthematicus,* are moderate-sized southern African monitors which become quite docile in captivity. Photo by H. Hansen, Aquarium Berlin.

Varanus salvadorii, the Papuan monitor, is usually found near water. Photo by Dr. O. Klee.

Klauberina riversiana, the island night lizard, occurs on the islands off the coast of southern California. From Van Denburgh.

Lepidophyma is the most widely distributed group, being absent only from the United States. The many species of this group are similar, and some may be a foot in length. The genus incorporates the *Gaigeia* of earlier authors.

Xantusia is most widespread in the U.S. and adjacent Mexico. These lizards rarely exceed five inches overall. They are commonly known as night lizards, which adequately describes the family's nocturnal habits. The genus *Klauberina* is similar and is found only on certain islands off the California coast.

All of the night lizards are nocturnal creatures. The eggs are small and similar to those of geckos. They are insectivorous, preferring soft-bodied prey such as moths.

Xenosauridae

A small group of less than a dozen forms comprising two genera. The limbs are well developed and pentadactyl. Osteoderms are present. Parietal single, with pineal foramen. The temporal arch is strong and has a dorsolateral keel. The tympanum may be exposed or concealed. Eyelids are well developed.

The genus *Xenosaurus* is indigenous to Central America and Mexico. The species grow to about fifteen inches maximum and in many ways resemble the night lizard genus *Lepidophyma*, save for the presence of eyelids. The head is triangular and the whole animal is somewhat compressed dorsally. The dorsal surface is covered by small fine conical scales intermixed with slightly larger tubercles. The ventral plates are square, smooth, and arranged in rows. The various species are found in deserts or forests. *Xenosaurus arboreus*, as the name implies, climbs the trees and bushes of its home. These lizards are insectivorous.

In China can be found the sole species of the other genus, this being *Shinisaurus crocodilurus*. Discovered in 1930, it remains today one of the rarest creatures in Western collections. It is known to average an overall length of eighteen inches. As the name implies, the tail is similar in appearance to that of a crocodile, the dorsal surface hosting two rows of enlarged scales which extend from the nape. The head of *Shinisaurus* is more of a cube-shaped affair than that of *Xenosaurus*. In *Shinisaurus*, too, the body is not so compressed as the Mexican genus but is more cylindrical.

A young golden monitor, *Varanus flavescens,* from India. With maturity the color will change to agree with the common name. Photo by H. Hansen, Aquarium Berlin.

Gerrhonotus kingi, the Arizona alligator lizard, is a limbed anguid. Notice the distinct lateral fold. This species will stand on its hind legs to "beg" for food. Photo by F.J. Dodd, Jr.

Legless lizards of several families look remarkably alike as they are generally modified for burrowing. This is *Ophisaurus apodus.* Photo by J.K. Langhammer.

Ophiodes, a limbless South American anguid. Photo by R.G. Tuck, Jr., courtesy U.S. National Mus.

Lacertidae

The typical lizards, whose family name means as much (*lacerta* is Latin for lizard). These lizards are an Old World family, being particularly abundant in Europe and Africa. *Takydromus sexlineatus* extends eastward into Southeast Asia. All the genera have limbs. The upper temporal fossa is roofed over or else greatly reduced. Osteoderms may occur on the head. The power of autotomy is present. Teeth hollow at the base. There are about twenty recognized genera.

Takydromus has a typical lacertilian body, but the tail may be several times the length of the head and body. *Acanthodactylus* has fringes on the toes to help it maneuver in the deserts of Africa and Arabia where it lives. The tiger lizards of

Europe and western Asia are the home of many species of wall lizards. This is *Lacerta sicula*. Photo by Dr. O. Klee.

Lacerta muralis, the European wall lizard. Photo by H. Hansen, Aquarium Berlin.

The island glass lizard, *Ophisaurus compressus,* restricted to the southeastern United States. Photo by F.J. Dodd, Jr.

Anniella pulchra, the California legless lizard, is now greatly reduced in numbers over much of its restricted range. Photo by J.T. Collins.

Lacerta lilfordi is restricted to the Balearic Islands in the Mediterranean off Spain. Lacertids need some vegetable matter in their diet. Photo by G. Marcuse.

the genus *Nucras* are very fancifully colored. The body and tail are cylindrical and the limbs short. The genus is African.

The lacertids range from within the Arctic Circle (one species) to the tropics. They coexist with man and dwell in the darkest recesses of Africa. A good many forms are found in Asia in those areas bordering the Indian Ocean. The predominantly European genus *Lacerta* includes many green forms, probably the reason why people generally regard lizards as "green things." *Lacerta vivipara* is a widespread form which gives birth to young in the cooler regions it inhabits, while it lays eggs in the warmer regions. *Lacerta ocellata* and *L. lepida* are very colorful members of the group. The latter is the family giant, growing to two feet in length. Most lacertids are carnivorous, but many will also accept plants.

Teiidae

Just as the Agamidae and Iguanidae are nearly identical except for the hemisphere which they inhabit and the tooth placement, so too is the case with the Lacertidae and the present family. Unlike the Lacertidae, the Teiidae has some genera devoid of limbs. The teeth are solid at the base. An upper temporal arch is present, except perhaps in limbless species. Osteoderms are usually absent. The family is strongest in numbers in South America, the Caribbean and Mexico, and but a single genus reaches the United States.

To this family belong some good sized creatures, not as large as the green iguana but perhaps bulkier. The two species

The caiman lizard, *Dracaena guianensis,* is noted for its ability to crush snails—fingers would be even easier to crush. *Handle with care.* Photo by G. Marcuse.

Only one genus of teiid, *Cnemidophorus*, enters the United States. *C. gularis* is a common and widespread western species. From Van Denburgh.

of *Dracaena* are aquatic forms. While little is known of *D. paraguyensis*, *D. guianensis* may approach a length of four feet. The tegus of the forests, genus *Tupinambis*, grow in excess of a yard. These lizards have often earned notorious reputations in their haunts as being hen-house raiders. Most teiids, however, are about a foot or less in length. A great many are but a few inches in length, giving them the nickname of "micro-teiids."

Teiids are liable to turn up anywhere. *Cnemidophorus* is primarily a grasslands or desert creature, while *Ameiva* is an island-hopper of the Caribbean. *Dracaena* is aquatic, while *Bachia* and *Ophiognomen* are semifossorial. At least one species is found in caves. This form, known from Trinidad, is a small enough beast but it may yet have a claim to fame based on a peculiar trait reported for it: it is said to be luminous. While many fishes are bioluminescent, no known terrestrial verte-brate is, except perchance *Proctoporus shreivei*. To my know-ledge no one interested in this peculiar trait has used this par-ticular species for experimental work, only the other similar members of the genus *Proctoporus*. If we can examine some live specimens of this animal, it may "illuminate" the whole matter once and for all!

The black tegu, *Tupinambis teguixin,* grows to about a yard in length and will eat almost any food. Photo by H. Schultz.

While few teiids are able to run far bipedally, they nevertheless represent some of the fleetest-footed lizards known. The American *Cnemidophorus* has earned the well deserved name of "racerunner." Even the large tegus can hustle when necessary. One that I have kept for some time can leap a good six feet, reaching a table top from the floor while a few feet away. I have seen some *Tupinambis* moving on their hindlimbs with the forebody held off the ground, but they were not running—I think a more descriptive term would be "staggering." Nevertheless, they were surefooted and well balanced. Almost all teiids will consume both animal and plant matter.

Cordylidae

Here is a family wholly confined to one continent, Africa including Madagascar. I include here the Gerrhosauridae of some authors as the two groups are obviously very closely related. Osteoderms present. Parasternum usually absent, as are planes of autotomy. The teeth are hollow at the base. Eyelids present. Tympanum exposed. Lateral fold usually present. Scalation usually keeled, tail of limbed forms spiny.

The family contains about 60 forms, the largest member being about two feet long. The genera *Chamaesura*, *Tetradactylus*, and *Paratetradactylus* are limbless or have greatly reduced limbs. The limbed forms are generally flattened dorsally and can secrete themselves into rock crevices.

Gerrhosaurus major, the African plated lizard. Unlike *Cordylus*, *Gerrhosaurus* lay eggs. Photo by G. Marcuse.

Species of *Cordylus* vary quite a bit in their armament. Above is *Cordylus coeruleopunctatus,* below is *C. giganteus.* Photos by G. Marcuse.

In *Platysaurus* the body is flattened, the sexes sometimes differ in color and pattern, and the body lacks large keeled scales except on the tail. Photo of *P. capensis* by G. Marcuse.

The armadillo lizards of the genus *Cordylus* are very spiny creatures but as a rule are quite small. As a defensive measure they take the spiny tail into their mouth and coil as an armadillo would. The result is a very spiny ball that even the toughest of predators would not want to try swallowing. Similarly, the *Gerrhosaurus* group may take the hind limb into the mouth, forming a large circle of lizard. It must be remembered that snakes are their primary enemies and a large round mass such as the lizard forms would be impossible for a snake to swallow.

These lizards are omnivorous, feeding on fruits and blossoms as well as insects. Some forms are viviparous.

Dibamidae

At the time of this writing work is being done to determine if the two similar groups formerly known as Dibamidae and Anelytropsidae should be united. Because they are so similar, I have decided to incorporate them here but will provide descriptions which divide the two genera. Functional limbs absent. Tongue short, slightly nicked, and covered with papillae. Palate toothless. Arches absent. Pelvic and pectoral girdles greatly reduced. Eyes and ears concealed by skin. Teeth few, recurved, conical.

The genus *Anelytropsis* contains one species, *A. papillosus*. Interorbital septum and columella cranii well developed. Premaxillary bone single. Osteoderms present. No sign of external limbs. This lizard is fossorial and is found in east-central Mexico. It is a fleshy brown above and yellowish below. It has been caught only a very few times and remains known from a dozen specimens. Its diet is suspected to consist of ants and termites.

Dibamus is a genus of some six species distributed in the East Indies between India and New Guinea. The interorbital septum and columella cranii are absent. Premaxillary paired. Osteoderms absent. Males have vestigial traces of hindlimbs. They are usually an olive drab color. These lizards are very slender bodied, secretive, forest-dwelling fossorial animals. They lay hard-shelled eggs, sometimes in communal sites, and are insect eaters.

Scincidae

Easily the largest lizard family in numbers, species, and range, skinks occur everywhere a lizard can, except in the sea. Skinks are unique among lizards in having a secondary palate. Osteoderms are present. Frontal bones distinct except in the Feylininae; this subfamily (often considered a full family, Feyliniidae) also lacks the jugal bone and is viviparous or oviparous. Skinks have movable eyelids, except for *Ablepharis*, which has a clear spectacle. In addition, the lizards formerly classified as the full family Feyliniidae are now included in the Scincidae by most herpetologists; this group includes forms lacking both functional eyes and eyelids. Ear openings are usually present, as is the power of autotomy. The scales are usually smooth with

Neoseps reynoldsi, the Florida sand skink, is a degenerate burrower. Photo by F.J. Dodd, Jr.

The incredible spined tail of *Egernia depressa,* a large Australian skink, makes it instantly recognizable. Photo by G. Marcuse.

Tiliqua casuarinae, the she-oak skink, is an elongate blue-tongued Australian species. Photo courtesy Australian Reptile Park.

The shinglebacked skink, *Trachydosaurus rugosus,* is about 20 inches long. The short blunt tail looks like a second head. Photo courtesy Australian Reptile Park.

Egernia major is another Australian skink with keeled scales. Photo courtesy Australian Reptile Park.

The blue-tongued skink, *Tiliqua scincoides,* requires a varied fruit and meat diet. Photo courtesy Australian Reptile Park.

Detail of the head of *Mabuya,* a typical skink from Africa. Photo by G. Marcuse.

Comparatively few lizards are banded like this *Lygosoma fasciolatum,* but instead have horizontally striped patterns. Photo courtesy Australian Reptile Park.

a clear luster, but some genera, notably *Trachydosaurus* and *Tribolonotus,* have rough or keeled scales. Many forms lack limbs or possess but one pair; there may be five or fewer fingers.

Probably the most problematic genus has been *Lygosoma,* practically world-wide in distribution and having all stages of limb development. The genus *Eumeces* is common in the United States and includes the golden Great Plains skink, *E. obsoleta,* a foot-long lizard of the central states. Australia's *Trachydosaurus rugosus* looks like an animated pair of pinecones, having large scales and a tail resembling the head. The family giant is *Corucia zebrata,* a two-foot long tree dweller of the Solomon Islands.

The skinks are active, often nervous lizards. They hide under large boulders or in other inaccessible spots but sometimes take to hilly woodsides. They are mainly insectivorous but many also eat plants.

Helodermatidae

Eyelids well developed. Ear exposed. Limbs well developed, pentadactyl, bearing strong claws. Head blunt. The body is stocky and bulky, the tail thick and short. Osteoderms are present. The lower teeth are grooved and venom glands are located in the posterior section of the lower jaw. The scales are non-overlapping, looking like Indian beadwork. The two species are oviparous and are confined to Arizona and western coastal Mexico. These are the only venomous lizards.

The Mexican beaded lizard, *Heloderma horridum,* the only poisonous lizard other than the Gila monster. Photo by Ross Allen.

The exact nature of the venom is not well known. It is apparently neurotoxic, causing paralysis, but a lethal dosage has not been universally agreed upon. Human fatalities have been few and were probably not attributable solely to the lizard, as the victims were usually well intoxicated by alcohol. In at least one death the nature of the victim, being juvenile, probably didn't help.

Lanthanotidae

Teeth not hollow. Ear concealed; eyelids present, the lower being clear. Tail longer than head and body, tapering. Six rows of enlarged tubercles along the dorsal surface, the dorsalmost pair running the length of the tail. Nostrils situated on upper surface of snout. Ventral scales squarish, arranged in rows.

Lanthanotus is considered by some herpetologists to be the closest living lizard relative of snakes. Photo by the author.

As everyone has a favorite something-or-other, this lizard is my personal favorite. Long thought to be a poisonous lizard allied to the Gila monster, the earless monitor, *Lanthanotus borneensis*, has recently become available for study. It is not poisonous, as was expected. It is, however, one of the most lethargic of known animals, barely moving but a few inches in captivity. While its natural habits are unknown, captives have been induced to accept egg yolk, fish, and earthworms. It does well in the water and may stay submerged for some time. The nostrils are specially equipped to close so that the animal is airtight while submerged. The tongue is bifid and is used in the

Earless monitors laok large head scales, have a small eye, have sphincter muscles to close the nostrils, and have a prehensile tail. Photo by the author.

same manner that a snake would, only slower. It is also a fossorial form, having been found underground as often as in water.

These lizards are nocturnal beasts, but even then they move very little. Although the eyelids are functional, the lizard almost always elects to view his world through the spectacle in the lower eyelid. The tail appears segmented and is somewhat prehensile; whether or not *Lanthanotus* climbs is unknown. The color is reddish brown above, while below it is mottled pale orange and yellow.

Varanidae

To this group belong the true monitors, the true giants among lizards. The largest living lizard is *Varanus komodoensis*, the Komodo dragon of Indonesia, while *Varanus salvator* may be as long, if not as heavy. At the other extreme are *Varanus brevicauda* and *V. gilleni*, both of Australia and both under a foot in length. In all monitors there are four powerful limbs equipped with five sharp claws. The eyelids are present and the ear is exposed. The snout and neck are long, as are the teeth. The tongue is long, bifid, and protrusible. The upper

The green tree monitor, *Varanus prasinus,* an Indonesian species with a prehensile tail. Photo by G. Marcuse.

The infrequently seen Spencer's goanna, *Varanus spenceri,* from Australia. This species has larger head scales than similar species and reaches two feet in length. Photo by Dr. O. Klee.

Varanus salvadorii, from New Guinea, may hold the title of the longest living monitor, although it is not so bulky as the Komodo dragon. Note the unique bulbous snout. Photo by Dr. O. Klee.

The swift-running Timor monitor, *Varanus timorensis,* is widespread from Indonesia to Australia. Photo by Dr. O. Klee.

The rough-necked monitor of Borneo, *Varanus rudicollis*, is easily recognized by the extremely thin snout, long nostril, and enlarged, keeled nuchal scales. Photo by Dr. O. Klee.

temporal arch is present. Osteoderms are greatly reduced or absent. Scalation is uniformly small and granular. The tail may be spiny or long and whip-like. The family consists of one genus, with nearly 60 varieties, found in Africa (except Madagascar), Asia, and Australia.

These lizards are active predators. They can run, swim, and climb well; many are excellent burrowers. When frightened in the open, they aim at clambering up the nearest vertical object, herpetologists not excepted! These animals are strictly carnivorous and strictly oviparous.

Anguinidae

With the exception of two genera, this is a New World group. *Anguis* inhabits Europe, while *Ophisaurus* makes its way through a good deal of the Old World, including Asia, but is absent from Australia and New Zealand. Arches are present. Osteoderms are usually present, as are autotomy planes. Tongue long, slightly bifid. Similar to the skinks except (mainly) for these points: secondary palate absent; parasternum absent; tongue not broad. Premaxillary single. Occipital bone universal.

Gerrhonotus multicarinatus, a common American alligator lizard. Photo by Muller Schmida.

Ophisaurus ventralis, the common glass lizard of the eastern United States, is often bright green in color. Photo courtesy American Mus. Nat. Hist.

There are many limbless forms in this family, including *Anguis* and *Ophisaurus*. *Ophiodes* is a New World limbless form, while the Caribbean *Wetmorena* has very small, thin limbs.

The alligator lizards, genus *Gerrhonotus*, have prehensile tails to facilitate climbing. These lizards make excellent pets and can be induced to stand on their hind legs and "beg" as a pet dog would. The galliwasps of the genus *Diploglossus* may be nearly two feet long. These stocky, skink-like lizards are nearly identical to the smaller *Wetmorena*, but while the former is pentadactyl, the latter is tetradactyl. The diminutive *Sauresia sepsoides* is another closely allied form.

The glass "snakes" of the *Ophisaurus* group have the widest distribution. There are four or five varieties in the United States, one in Europe and Russia, and one in China. The little *Ophiodes* are similar but have flap-like hind limbs; as these are essentially useless, I refer to the genus above as "limbless."

Anniellidae

This small family has not yet been seriously allied with any other group, so it maintains the distinctiveness of its own family status. There are but two species, one with two subspecies, found only in California and Baja California. They are limbless lizards lacking an external ear but possessing eyelids and functional eyes. They are very thin bodied, and a giant may be nine inches long. The upper temporal arch is absent. Osteoderms reduced, the scales smooth and subequal. The head is conical, the upper jaw extending far beyond the lower. The tongue is smooth, dark, bifid, and protrusible. Columella cranii absent.

Anniella pulchra, a diminutive burrower, is rarely seen in captivity. There are functional eyelids, but no external ear openings. From Van Denburgh.

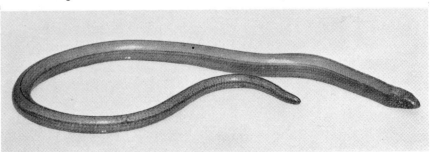

Teeth few, large, recurved, resembling those of *Heloderma*. The taxa are as follows: silvery legless lizard, *Anniella pulchra pulchra*; black legless lizard, *A. pulchra nigra*; and Geronimo legless lizard, *A. geronimensis*.

These lizards are fossorial and prefer loose soil near moisture, such as beaches. They feed on small invertebrate animals including earthworms. The species are known to be viviparous.

Glossary

Amniote egg: An egg which contains the embryo in a fluid-filled cavity during development. Such a mechanism is found only in reptiles, birds, and mammals. The membrane which envelopes the cavity is called the amnion.

Arches: Skeletal bridges found in the skull. These arches underlie the region for which they are named. Absent in lizards is the arch formed by the jugal and quadrate bones. This feature is present in the similar tuatara (*Sphenodon punctatus*) of New Zealand. The arch most typically found in lizards is the temporal arch, formed from the squamosal and postorbital bones.

Atlas: The first vertebral segment, articulating directly to the skull at the occipital condyle.

Axis: The second vertebral segment, which is responsible for the movement of the skull.

Columella cranii: Also known as epipterygoid bone, a rodlike pair of thin shafts found on either side of the braincase.

Crepuscular: Active by dusk or dawn.

Diurnal: Active by day.

Fossorial: Being by nature a burrowing animal.

Homeostasis: The metabolic balancing of bodily functions to a normal state of operation. For example, maintenance of body temperature, water retention, etc.

Jacobson's organ: A paired sensory mechanism found in the roof of the mouth in certain reptiles. Air particles from outside are brought by the tongue to this organ for analysis. It is essentially an extension of the sense of smell.

Lateral fold: The long margin along the body of certain lizards whose skin contains osteoderms, such as *Ophisaurus* and *Gerrhosaurus*. The fold region is devoid of osteoderms, allowing bodily growth.

Nocturnal: Active by night.

Occipital condyle: The point at the rear of the skull to which the vertebral column attaches. In reptiles the condyle is single; in amphibians it is paired.

Pentadactyl: Having five digits.

Secondary palate: A bony reinforcement along the roof of the mouth, found principally in skinks.

Temporal fossa: The opening found behind the eye in the skull. In some forms the fossa is roofed over by bone, while in others it exists as a large gap, frequently bordered inferiorly by a temporal arch.

Zygantra: A pair of recesses in the vertebrae of snakes into which the paired zygosphenes insert.

Zygosphenes: Paired projections located on the posterior surface of the vertebrae of snakes. These insert into the zygantra to prevent the serpent's body from twisting on its axis. These processes are generally not found in lizards.

Bibliography

This is a selected bibliography presenting as wide a variety of geographic and family material as possible. A great many other references can be found in most.

JOURNALS:

Herpetologica, published quarterly by the Herpetologists' League.

Copeia, published quarterly by the American Society of Ichthyologists and Herpetologists.

Journal of Herpetology, published by the Society for the Study of Amphibians and Reptiles.

BOOKS AND ARTICLES:

Anderson, L.G., 1914. "A new *Telmatobius* and new Teiid lizards from South America," *Arkiv fur Zool.*, Band 9, no. 3, pp. 1-12.

Anderson, S., 1963. "Amphibians & Reptiles from Iran," *Proc. Cal. Acad. Sci.*, vol. 31, no. 16.

Angel, F., 1942. "Les Lezards de Madagascar," *Mem. Acad. Melgache*, vol. 36.

Bellairs, A., 1970. *The Life of Reptiles*. 2 vols. Universe Nat. Hist. Ser.

Bogert, C.M. & R.M. del Campo, 1960. "The Gila Monster and its Allies," *Bull. Amer. Mus. Nat. Hist.*, vol. 109, art. 1.

Boulenger, G.A., 1885-87. *Catalogue of the Lizards in the British Museum (Natural History)*. Vols. i-iii.

Burt, C.E. & M. Burt, 1931. "South American Lizards in the collection of the American Museum of Natural History," *Bull. Amer. Mus. Nat. Hist.*, vol. 61, art. 7.

Cochran, D.M., 1941. "The Herpetology of Hispaniola," *Bull. U.S. Nat'l. Mus.*, no. 177. Washington, D.C.

Cope, E.D., 1885. "A contribution to the herpetology of Mexico," *Proc. Amer. Phil. Soc.*, vol. 22, part 4.

Davey, K., 1971. *Australian Lizards*. Periwinkle Books.

Del Toro, M.A., 1960. *Los Reptiles de Chiapas*. Inst. Zool. Del Estado.

Deraniyagala, P.E.P.; 1953. *A Color Atlas of some Vertebrate Animals from Ceylon*. Vol. ii. Ceylon Gov't. Printing Off.

De Rooij, N., 1914. *Reptiles of the Indo-Australian Archipelago*. Leiden.

Ditmars, R.L., 1933. *Reptiles of the World*. McMillan.

Dixon, J.R., 1973. "A systematic review of the Teiid lizards, genus *Bachia*," *Univ. Kansas Mus. Nat. Hist., Misc. Publ.* 57.

Donoso-Barros, R., 1966. *Reptiles de Chile*. Univ. de Chile.

Echternacht, A., 1971. "Middle American lizards of the genus *Ameiva*," *Univ. Kansas Mus. Nat. Hist., Misc. Publ.* 55.

Fitch, H.S., 1954. "Life history and ecology of the five-lined skink, *Eumeces fasciatus*, " *Univ. Kansas Publ., Mus. Nat. Hist.*, vol. 8, no. 1.

————, 1954. "An ecological study of the collared lizard, *Crotaphytus collaris*," *ibid*, vol. 8, no. 3.

Gadow, H., 1901. *Amphibia and Reptiles*. Vol. viii. Cambridge Nat. Hist. Ser.

Greer,. A., 1970. "A subfamilial classification of scincid lizards," *Bull. Mus. Comp. Zool., Harvard*, vol. 139, no. 3.

McDowell, S.B. & C.M. Bogert, 1954. "The systematic position of *Lanthanotus*, and the affinities of the Anguinomorphan lizards," *Bull. Amer. Mus. Nat. Hist.*, vol. 105, art. 1.

Mertens, R.F., 1942. *Die Familie der Warane*. Senck. Natur. Gesell.

Milstead, W., 1965. *Lizard ecology: a symposium*. Univ. Missouri Press.

Mittleman, M., 1952. "A generic synopsis of the lizards of the subfamily Lygosominae," *Smithsonian Misc. Coll.*, vol. 117, no. 17.

Montanucci, R., 1973. "Systematics and evolution of the Andean lizard genus *Pholidobolus* (Sauria: Teiidae)," *Univ. Kansas Mus. Nat. Hist., Misc. Publ.* 59.

Pope, C.H., 1936. *The Reptile World.* Knopf.

Romer, A.S., 1933. *The Vertebrate Story.* Univ. Chicago Press.

Rose, W., 1962. *Reptiles and amphibians of southern Africa.* Maskew-Miller.

Roth, W. & C. Gans, 1960. "The luminous organs of *Proctoporus*," *Breviora, Mus. Comp. Zool.*, no. 125.

Schmidt, K.P., 1909. "Contribution to the Herpetology of the Belgian Congo," *Bull. Amer. Mus. Nat. Hist.*, vol. 39.

_____, & R.F. Inger, 1957. *Living Reptiles of the World.* Doubleday.

Sharell, R., 1966. *The Tuatara, Lizards and Frogs of New Zealand.* Collins.

Shaw, C.E., 1966. "A boon from Borneo," *Zoonooz*, San Diego Zool. Soc.

Simms, C., 1970. *Lives of British Lizards.* Goose & Sons.

Smith, H.M., 1935. "Miscellaneous notes on Mexican lizards," *Univ. Kansas Sci. Bull.*, vol. 22, no. 6.

_____, 1946. *Handbook of lizards of the United States and of Canada.* Comstock Press.

Taylor, E.H., 1963. "The lizards of Thailand," *Univ. Kansas Sci. Bull.*, vol. 44.

Waite, E.R., 1929. *The reptiles and amphibians of South Australia,* Harrison Weir, Adelaide.

Worrell, E., 1966. *Reptiles of Australia.* Angus and Robertson.

Zweifel, R.G. & C.H. Lowe, 1966. "The ecology of a population of *Xantusia vigilis*," *Amer. Mus. Novitates*, no. 2247.

Index

Illustrations are in **bold** type.